How To Be Friends With Yourself & Your Family

How To Be Friends With Yourself & Your Family

Jean Rosenbaum, M.D.

Book design by Robert Stevenson

SBN 0-912228-33-4

Printed in the U.S.A.

Introduction

Introduction

Jean Rosenbaum, M.D.

It is common in our technological society to easily obtain information on how to do or get anything in the material world. This applies to money, goods and luxuries of every sort.

In the world of people there are also an enormous variety of books and magazines devoted to improving one's status: how to handle this one, impress that one, influence them or enjoy whatever better.

In the meantime the decline in family life in America since World War II has been enormous and disastrous. The impact of this destruction of the nuclear human relationship is so great it will take decades of sociologists and psychologists to calculate.

Now there is nothing wrong with having money, enjoying things and being successfully involved with people. There is something wrong if all of that does not revolve around what should be the most significant of people relationships—namely, your family.

If you are the most popular person in Hollywood and don't enjoy your family, you are nowhere.

If you are a billionaire and die alone without anyone who cares, you are an emotionally bankrupt human being.

The purpose of this book is to turn folks' attention to the primary human relationship in anyone's life, and how to improve that relationship.

Yes, it is healthy to like yourself. Indeed, this is vital in order to accomplish the other intent of this work. For if you don't like yourself you will find that it's impossible to like anyone else. Like yourself, sure, but you must also learn to like your family.

The family is and will be your number one priority among significant relationships. So not only like your family but love and enjoy them as well.

I am quite aware that such an achievement is difficult in our complex society but I'm sure you will agree with its importance.

There are steps to expanding and enjoying family life. They may be different than what you are accustomed to but they are not difficult.

Join me then in this friendly handbook on how to make friends with your family.

How to Live With Yourself and Like It

What kind of a person are you? It can be put another way also—What kind of a self do you have?

Jane, a patient with personality problems to whom I put this same question, bristled as she replied, "I am myself — the way I was born —and people will just have to learn to accept me as I am!"

There were several fallacies in Jane's statement, and her ideas of selfhood were slowly changed over a long period of psychoanalysis.

First, I pointed out to her that the self is not something which you are automatically assigned at birth. The self is partly, at least, a created condition of personality which is our personal responsibility. You, as an individual, determine whether that self shall be productive or sterile, powerful or weak, happy or miserable.

You determine this in a variety of ways. The interests that you develop, the thoughts you have (both the conscious ones and those you attempt to deny), the ideals that you hold in front of yourself, and the varying ways in which you react emotionally to situations are all important aspects of the self-molding process.

While emphasizing one's personal responsibility for self-development, the influence which other people have on a person's self-image cannot be discounted. Many times the level of your self-esteem will rise or fall depending upon what others say about or to you.

A compliment or an expression of confidence will increase your self-esteem. A reprimand or criticism may lower it. You, as a person, will reflect this in your actions and appearance. Thus, the self is built from within and also from outside contacts and influences.

Thus, as Jane came to see and understand, the self is created, and the process of creation is continuous. Each day as you live the self is being slowly altered. It is up to you to determine whether that alteration is good or bad — in terms of personality adjustment.

Jane, who had insisted that people would have to learn to accept her as she was, finally admitted that she really didn't like herself very well.

"How do you expect others to live with you if you can't live with yourself?" I asked her. She had never thought of it that way. She was asking others to do what she could not begin to do herself.

Every self-resentment Jane had ever felt she still carried. Every slight she thought she had ever received she remembered. Her mind was filled with a series of petty annoyances and grudges.

She was disagreeable to others and to herself because she had convinced herself that this was her real personality. She didn't like it. That's why she came to me for help.

Jane was eventually able to learn that instead of breaking down the self, she could build the self up into a person that was pleasing to herself and others. When she achieved that goal, she was able to live with herself.

Jane had made a common mistake when she expected other people to like her even when she could not like herself. This is an immature attitude. It is like the mother-infant relationship. A mother has to love and feed a child. But peers do not have to give respect and affection. When they do, they expect something in return.

Self-Esteem: Key to Living With Yourself

Several years ago a young bride came to me for consultation. Her husband, she explained, was not making her happy. When I asked her for specific complaints about him, she could only repeat that he was not making her happy.

"Were you happier before you met your husband?" I asked her.

"Of course not," she replied, "that's why I married him—for him to make me happy!"'

At the time she consulted me, she was tempted to have an affair with a man she worked with. Because in his superficial dealings with her he smiled a lot and joked, she felt that he was trying to show that he loved her.

The person who has no esteem for himself cannot be sustained indefinitely by other people's attentions. Consequently, nothing reveals the lack of self-esteem more quickly than an enforced idleness or aloneness.

Traditionally, great men, especially religious leaders, have sought isolation in order to renew themselves. Jesus spent time in the wilderness. Moses went to the mountaintop. New strength and a source of inspiration was found by spending time in isolated places where they could freely commune with God without the distractions of the everyday world.

To many, however, the busy everyday world is the only thing that stands between them and the misery of themselves.

I once counseled a middle-aged professional man who was well known in town for his many civic and social responsibilities. Even in an age of action, Allan was hyperactive, rushing from one project or meeting to the next. Much of this activity was in connection with his profession, and thus the time could be justified in his eyes and in the eyes of his family, whom he seldom saw.

A minor physical illness occurred and he had to stop working for a brief period and curtail his other activities. He'll get a much needed rest, his family and friends thought. But one day when his wife went out to shop and he was left alone, Allan panicked.

The basic irrational fear from which he suffered was that he was a real person only in terms of what he did. Alone and inactive, faced with his own internal thoughts, Allan felt that there was no interior person. He was, in his own feelings, only a man of straw.

Hiding One's Real Self

Another problem of selfhood is that of persons who are afraid to let others know their real selves.

Elizabeth, a young attractive woman, was able to relate to other people only on a superficial social basis. Although she dated regularly, she was not able to share her thoughts and feelings with anyone. Whenever she felt that another person was getting too close to her, she would find some pretext for breaking off the relationship.

Since she pictured herself as a very shallow person, she feared that if anyone got to know her, he would despise her. Where had she gotten such a picture? One source for this low measure of self-esteem was a teacher, a woman whom Elizabeth had greatly admired.

"I looked up to her," Elizabeth explained. "I thought she was one of the most brilliant people I had ever met. She seemed to know something about everything. When she asked me to be on a school debate team that she was sponsoring, I was thrilled."

Unfortunately the teacher's tact did not match her intelligence. She became increasingly critical of all the students but especially of Elizabeth. Her demands for perfection were far beyond the capabilities of the young people on the debate team.

"I got more and more nervous," admitted Elizabeth. "I had always thought I was a special favorite of hers, so it was harder for me to take her sarcastic remarks. One day, however, I just couldn't take it anymore. She had scolded me for not being better prepared with my material for the debate. I couldn't help myself; I burst into tears. This really made her angry and she dismissed me from the team. She called me a silly and shallow girl."

This unhappy and traumatic experience had left its mark on Elizabeth and made it difficult for her to be friends with other people. She was, obviously, afraid of a repetition of the teacher's accusation of "silly and shallow."

She took refuge in a very active social life. She could dance, discuss the details of current student activities or trends in movies. But let anyone ask her how she felt about these things, and she immediately became very defensive and would not give a direct answer.

Elizabeth slowly learned to accept a better and more accurate evaluation of her personality. She was encouraged to share her ideas with others.

To make it easier for her at the beginning, I had her write down her thoughts, feelings and opinions. These she would read aloud to me. That was the first step.

In the second step, we would discuss her opinions. Soon she was able to verbalize her thoughts and even initiate topics of importance. Each such session was a way of building up Elizabeth's self-esteem and changing her mental picture of herself.

Later she was able to relate socially and emotionally to others. She knew and accepted the picture of herself as a likable and interesting individual. Elizabeth's life changed for the better as she met and acquired new and close friends.

Re-Creating Your Personality

We have seen what goes into the making of the self. The self you develop determines whether you are going to live in serenity or in constant anxiety.

But if you are dissatisfied with present self-development, how can you remake yourself? It is not an easy or casual task, yet it is possible. All the people I have mentioned did — in the long run — learn to remake their personalities so they could live with themselves.

There is the well-known biblical injunction, "You must be born anew." This can certainly be interpreted as a mandate to re-create yourself, your personality.

The first step is to look honestly and objectively at yourself. Do you like what you see? Do you really like living with yourself? Do you know how to live?

These will be, no doubt in most cases, painful questions. However, unless you answer them truthfully, you cannot start to remake yourself.

The next step is to ask yourself why you are the way you are. What things and particularly what people have influenced you?

Hero worship is common to all ages. Young people often admire popular singers or movie stars. Sometimes it is a parent or other relative who is admired. It may be a teacher or a fellow student. Adults continue, though to a lesser degree, this same hero worship. Political figures, successful businessmen and scientists are admired for their traits of leadership and enterprise.

Another term for a hero figure is an ego ideal. We all have ego ideals. They play a necessary role in developing a self-concept.

As children we tend to make our parents our ego ideals. This is the natural result of the family living unit. Sometimes, however, parents may have inculcated negative identifications that no longer function in adult life or under present conditions. The wise individual knows that to be a really mature, well-adjusted person, he must reassess those earlier identifications and discard what is harmful or no longer valid.

Parents sometimes have overemphasized the *don'ts* instead of carefully blending the necessary discipline and creative freedom. They may have held up as examples persons of limited appeal, or they may not have taken into account the personal characteristics of their children.

"My father thought that you were shiftless if you did not own your own home," a businessman confessed to me, "and it took me a long time to get over feelings of guilt because I was a renter. My wife and I happen to prefer to live in an apartment."

As adults we can choose new identifications that are more suited to our present needs. Many persons study the biographies of great people in an attempt to imitate them.

Orphans who have no family to look up to emulate famous people and, through substitution, pattern their lives upon these strangers.

Nearly every successful person has studied the biographies of important people who have met the challenges of life. In psychiatry this identification is well known. It is a principle that the person we identify with, we become. This, of course, leads us to some problems of identification. Some people set their goals too high, beyond their capacity.

Sam suffered a nervous breakdown when he failed to pass some of his college examinations. Analysis revealed that his hero was a professor prominent in the particular field of mathematics which Sam was studying. Unfortunately, Sam did not have the capacity to work successfully in this highly complicated discipline. He was unable to acknowledge his limitations or to face his failure.

It was only when he was able to recognize his own capabilities and to substitute more realistic hero figures that Sam could regain his mental health. Incidentally, he achieved success and satisfaction in another occupation for which he was more suited.

On the other hand, you should not set your goals too low by identifying beneath your abilities. If you are more successful than your ego ideal, you will also feel uncomfortable.

This has sometimes been true of the children of immigrants who were illiterate or unfamiliar with American ways. In achieving a superior intellectual development, the children often suffered from feelings of guilt. They had the idea that by their very success they were putting their parents down.

Thoughts Which Build Self-Esteem

A third and final step in remaking yourself is to control your emotions and to cultivate the thoughts that will build self-esteem.

There is a direct connection between your emotions and thoughts. In a sense, they interrelate. You cannot separate the two. You think "X" and you immediately respond with a matching "X" feeling. You may also experience an "X" emotion and then think an "X" thought. One will trigger the other.

Therefore, it is important to have control over both your emotions and your thoughts. For example, you may experience a disappointment in some plans. The thought of this disappointment lodges in your mind and colors all of your emotional attitudes. You may fail to see some other opportunity because of this emphasis in your thinking. Your thoughts and emotions have narrowed into a small focus.

The person who thinks emotionally about resentments and criticisms limits his or her development as a person.

It has long been said, "You are what you eat." It can also be said, "You are what you think." Your personality and actions are the result of your plans and thoughts. If you have only negative thoughts and emotions, your self-esteem will be lowered.

You can build your self-esteem by emphasizing positive and creative thoughts. Start out now by making a list of those things which will raise your self-esteem. Recall previous accomplishments, compliments you have received and other achievements. Knowing that you have been successful in the past will help you meet and solve the problems of the present.

Don't let negative emotions limit you. I can think of any number of cases where individuals never were able to realize their fullest potential because they chose to see only the worst in themselves and others.

A woman I knew carried a deep resentment within her which had seriously handicapped her personality. This resentment was directed against her sister. "She always got the best of things," she complained. "She had piano lessons. She got to go to camp. She went on to college, and I didn't."

The truth was that this woman had enjoyed the same opportunities as her sister, but out of resentment had refused to accept them. She did not love herself as a person and made it difficult for others to love her.

You can only grow as a person if you permit yourself to expand in the direction of the best you are capable of performing.

Living with yourself in comfort and pleasure may be a challenge to you. But it is a challenge that you can successfully meet. When you can live with yourself and like it, then you will find that your family, as well as others, will enjoy living with you also.

How To Be Friends With Your Family

After you feel comfortable living with yourself, you have to ask whether others feel comfortable living with you! More specifically, is your family at ease living with you?

One of the basic problems for many of us is that we don't treat as friends the members of our family. The family relationship many times blocks out their real personalities—personalities we would find very interesting in strangers. Mother, father, sister, brother, daughter and son can be mere labels unless we see the person behind the title. Unless there is a genuine effort to know and share with each other, "family" can mean just a group of people under the same roof, using the same address. Each member of the family should be willing to take the initiative. In other words, the family effort begins with *you*.

You should apply the same intelligence to family living that you apply to your business, profession or other interests. You should be friends with your family and treat them with the same consideration and respect with which you treat your other friends. Being yourself may be bad if it means being selfish and inconsiderate. You may find that you are using your family unfairly, that you are making them put up with the worst side of your nature while you present the best side to others outside the immediate family circle.

Hugh's family were finding him more and more difficult to live with since he had gotten more involved in his business. His wife was lonely and depressed. The thought of getting a divorce nagged her. "Hugh has changed," she told me. "I'm not able to really talk to him anymore. Yet when we're out he treats other people with consideration and kindness. It's just at home that he behaves so badly."

His children avoided him whenever possible. "Dad's always yelling at me for some reason or other," his older boy said. "Last week he even slapped my little sister, just because he said she was playing her stereo loud."

When questioned about his behavior and his attitude, Hugh was defensive. "It's my home, so why can't I act like myself? I beat my brains out all day long to provide well for them. They should be willing to put up with me. Isn't that what a family is for, after all?"

Hugh almost learned the hard way that that is not what a family is for. It is not a psychological punching bag that we can use to work off tensions. He had to learn that acting like himself, if it meant acting mean and inconsiderate, was not the way to treat your family. When he faced up to the way he was acting at home, Hugh admitted that he was wrong. "I would never put up with that kind of behavior from friends or business associates," he said, "nor do I act that way at work."

He saved his marriage and regained the affection and respect of his family by being willing to give them the best of his nature instead of the worst. He learned the difference between self-indulgence and self-discipline.

Many people, like Hugh, feel that they can let themselves go when at home. By letting themselves go, I mean letting go by having temper tantrums, selfish demands, and emotional moods. They behave like spoiled, undisciplined children and then wonder why they have family problems.

Transference: A Very Common Problem

One of your difficulties in giving your best to your family may be the psychological problem of transference. When transference occurs you may indulge in inappropriate anger. Transference is the redirection of emotions to people other than the original ones for whom they were intended, and inappropriate anger is anger which is out of proportion to the supposed cause or offense. It is "blowing up" at some trivial cause or because of some minor incident.

Here is the way transference can work in the family scene. Junior's team loses in Little League play and he is disappointed and angry. When he comes home and his mother asks him to put away his things, he answers her back and after a few explosive words, he is sent to his room.

Or, Junior's mother may have had a difficult day. She has a headache, the washing machine broke down, and just before getting supper she discovered that she is out of milk. If she is emotionally upset, she may transfer her feelings of anger at these inanimate things to the object that next crosses her path. It may be one of her children, her husband or the family pet. In any case, she will have temporarily relieved her feelings, but the other person will be bewildered and resentful.

Frequently family fights and problems, as a result of transference, happen when the working members of the family return home still seething with the frustrations and resentments of their work lives. For example, a husband and father has a disagreement with his boss, but he cannot say anything to him because he doesn't want to risk losing his job. That undischarged anger is still seething inside when he arrives home.

As he pulls into the drive, he sees that his son has not put away his bicycle as he had been told to do. The father bursts into the house in a rage and screams at his son. He has transferred the anger he feels toward his boss to his son. In doing this, he has rid himself of his anger but created a new situation of family anxiety and tenseness. In other words, he has acted like a good employee but as a bad father. And he certainly has not acted like a mature adult!

If he had been a mature adult he would have been able to handle his disagreement with his boss in a less emotional way and not have allowed it to influence his attitude and actions at home. Although he may have arrived home still angry over what had happened at work, he would have been adult and mature enough to realize that the anger he felt when he saw his son's bicycle was simply an excuse for him to express his unresolved anger with his boss.

It is necessary to understand the causes of anger so that you are able to control the way you express it. In a practical way, the father described above should have refrained from telling his son about the bicycle until after he cooled down from the office episode. To help him drain off that excess anger, he should have gotten busy with a task that required some physical effort, such as mowing the lawn. Or if it helped him to talk out the situation, he should have sat down and told his wife about the incident at the office.

For some people, just being able to tell things to a sympathetic and understanding person is enough, but for others, it helps to be busy doing something. A man I know once told me that the year he worked at a job which he didn't like and which made him angry, he also had the cleanest garage in town. "Every time I got angry, I came home and cleaned out the garage. By the time I had finished it and taken stuff to the dump, I was feeling more like myself again," he explained.

Cooling Off

It is important to learn what type of action you should take to get rid of your anger in an acceptable fashion without making others suffer for it. The next time you have the impulse to let go and relieve yourself of your feelings at the expense of a member of your family, ask yourself if this is really an appropriate action. Perhaps you are having a temper transference problem.

This does not mean that anger will never arise within the family. Conflict will occur, but it can be handled in two ways. One way is to take some preventive measures; another way is to decide to handle heated exchanges in an emotionally mature way. A good way is to have a combination of these two methods. When you can do this, you are giving your best to your family.

In a preventive way, you can do your part to keep down the hostile climate in your family environment. Hostility may arise because of feelings of rivalry, resentment, jealousy or frustration. These feelings may be experienced by any member of the family group and may involve interaction between any members. This can often be best handled if you treat these feelings in the family as you would treat them in an outside group. By applying the same tact and measure of understanding, you not only can solve the problems of these feelings, but in most cases you can prevent them from ever coming to the problem stage.

There are times when it is important to show more than tact. You can show consideration by giving

other family members a chance to air their griev-
ances and anger in ways that are acceptable and
not damaging to family relationships or loyalties.
You can do this by bringing up the subject in some
suitable way, such as: "You look as if you are really
angry at the world. Has something happened?" or
"Do you have a problem?" Often all the other person needs is an invitation to share his problem and
perhaps to receive some help in solving it.

The thing you must avoid is a false stoical attitude
in which everyone goes around with a stiff upper
lip and a smoldering fire of anger inside. Family
members should rather be encouraged to talk out
tensions and discuss their reasons for feeling irri-
tated and upset. Each person in the family should
be concerned enough to be alert to the moods of
the others, so that he or she knows when to offer
helpful counsel and when to listen. In any case, an
invitation to discuss a real or imagined wrong
should never be followed by words of condemna-
tion or acts of punishment.

One man whom I treated in analysis was suffering
from a variety of anxiety symptoms because he was
unable to stop his worrying and his easily aroused
feelings of irritation. Since his wife had implied
that she was concerned and wanted to help him, I
asked him why he had not confided in her. He
replied that it was very difficult for him to talk
things over with another person. During the course
of his treatment it was revealed that as a boy his
parents had encouraged him to talk over things
with them but if it was something they did not
approve of, he was punished. He consequently

built up a distrust of other people even when he knew that they were trying to help him. He had not even been able to bring himself to the point of seeking help from a psychiatrist until his health began to deteriorate.

Creating a Positive Mood

In any family situation it usually takes only one person to start the ball rolling by showing consideration, tact and understanding. Soon all the family members are responding in a similarly positive fashion, until giving your best and doing your best becomes a family habit and a family trait.

Consideration within the family is not only necessary for family harmony, but it is also an essential ingredient in any recipe for family happiness. What happens when you emphasize consideration? For one thing, it means getting rid of the irritations that may be causing family trouble. It means breaking the habit of getting annoyed easily and quickly. It means eliminating periods of sulkiness and grudge-keeping. Consideration can made that difference between unhappiness and happiness in your family life.

The best rule for consideration is still the golden rule. Too many people seem to think that it applies only to their attitude and conduct toward friends or strangers. It should first and always be applied to your home and family. If you can learn to treat each member of your family as you would like to be treated, you will find that there will be a marked upswing in your family happiness.

However there is more to the golden rule t̶̶̶ ̶̶̶̶̶̶. It also means learning to use empathy in your relationships with other people. Empathy is using your understanding and imagination to put yourself in another's place. It is easier to get along with other people when you learn to develop a sympathetic understanding of what they are feeling and experiencing.

How do you learn to develop empathy? You start by having a genuine interest in other people and a real concern for them and what they are feeling and experiencing in their lives. It is really a form of role-playing in which you temporarily put yourself in the other person's shoes and try to identify with him. It means putting aside for the moment your own selfishness, your own personal interests, your biases and prejudices, and looking at others with sympathetic understanding. Empathy means that you can say to another person, "I know just how you feel," and mean it.

As a parent, it means that you can have a better understanding of your children. Losing a Little League game may not seem so important to you; but if you try to understand the relative importance of this in your son's life, you will be able to share and help him cope with his disappointment. As an adult, you may feel impatient with your daughter's tears at not being asked to a school dance. But again, with empathy, you will be able to offer the right amount of sympathetic understanding.

Wives need to understand the problems and frustrations faced by their husbands, and husbands need to be cognizant of the many frustrations that come to the wife who is at home each day keeping house and handling family problems by herself. Empathy is one way of giving your best.

No Double Standard

"Our marriage and family life have been happy and without serious problems because of our emphasis on mutual consideration," explained one of my clients. "My husband and I resolved that we would never allow habits of rudeness, unconcern or thoughtlessness to become our family habits. We have taught our children this and we think that it has made them happier individuals as well as children whom we enjoy living with."

You give your best to your family when you do not impose upon them. No one likes to be imposed upon; it is irritating to nearly everyone. Frequently, however, people who would never dream of imposing on other people will have no hesitation about imposing upon members of their family. In other words, they have a double standard.

You impose on your family when you are late for meals or have fussy and demanding eating habits. You impose when you refuse to be neat at home and expect others in the family to wait on you. You impose when you expect your family to put up with your unreasonable moods.

When you give your best to your family, you do not try to enforce your views, desires and plans on them at the expense of other family members. You keep up your personal appearance at home and in front of your family. You have good manners at home just as you have good manners when you are out in public.

Affection, concern, and expression of love and understanding all go into the making of a successful and happy family relationship. A child from a happy family usually has a better chance of achieving happiness in his adult life. A man or woman from a happy family usually enjoys his or her job more and is more successful in what he or she chooses to do.

A happy family does not come about by accident. It is the result of a plan carried out by all members of the family. It comes from each member doing his best for the family. Because the family is so important, we cannot afford to wait until it has been ruptured by outward events before taking steps to renew and strengthen family life.

You can preserve the unity of your family by your attitude toward family living. Much of your personal happiness depends on how well you get along with your family; your family are your most important friends. Learning how to make friends with your family and to keep them as your friends is a life-long project.

In the first two chapters of this book we have described wholesome living with yourself and your family. Now we shall narrow in on several common sources of unhappiness and discuss how to deal with them.

Facing Your Fear

We can be trying hard to live with ourselves and our families, yet beneath the surface we may be struggling with emotions we have not recognized or dealt with. Fear is one of these emotions we are often reluctant to admit even to ourselves. Learning to face our fears can greatly increase our personal and family happiness.

Though frequently we don't realize it, fear can be beneficial to us. It can move us to slow down on a hazardous highway or to keep our distance from an exposed electrical wire or to throw away the suspicious-smelling potato salad.

But more often fear is a negative emotion which uselessly wastes our energy and prevents us from enjoying the moment or the day. Unless we learn how to master our fears and handle fear situations, our happiness and even our health can suffer.

If the only instigators of fear were obvious, external dangers, it would not present a problem for most of us. But the sources of fear are not that simple. The fears that rise from within us with no recognizable external cause are the most troublesome. Fear is not a simple emotion. It has many facets and sometimes surprisingly deep roots.

Fear shows itself in two main ways: physically and psychologically. We all have experienced the bodily reactions that fear can trigger. The heart beats faster or irregularly. One may have gastrointestinal symptoms such as vomiting or diarrhea. Many people when afraid become short of breath or feel unable to breathe properly. Others experience chest pains and nervous tremors.

Fear also manifests itself psychologically. It can so fire one's emotions as to lead to sudden, wrong decisions. It can inhibit one from expressing his ideas or feelings or taking needed action. It can be accompanied by anxiety or even outright panic.

Realistic Expectations

Before we talk about some of the common causes of fears and how to handle them, we should banish any unrealistic expectations that we can totally eliminate the causes of fear in our lives. Each day we face new situations, new problems and new people. Any or all of these have the potential of exciting some degree of fear. A young salesman about to call on an important buyer who has the reputation of being a "bear" is understandably apprehensive. The housewife giving her first speech before the ladies' society should expect to be nervous. If either the salesman or the housewife is so overwhelmed by fear that they are unable to go on with the show, then they'll want to do something about this fear.

Once we have learned through experience to recognize the beginning signs of fear, we have the edge because we are forewarned. You might say that the individual and his fear are facing each other as opponents in a fight from which only one can emerge a winner. The person has an advantage because he can prepare himself psychologically and emotionally for the battle.

The Unknown

One of the first things to do in preparing yourself for battle with fear is to acquaint yourself with the common sources of fear. It helps to know you are not alone in your fears. Others are frightened by the same situations.

The unknown is a chief source of fear. Livy said thousands of years ago, "We fear things in proportion to our ignorance of them." We all tend to fear what we don't know. This is a very natural reaction but not necessarily a mature one. Children and primitive peoples can be completely demoralized by their fears of the unknown. Ignorance lets the imagination run wild with no regard for reality. As we grow in knowledge and experience, we can better cope with the unknown. For example, fear of the dark is a basic, primitive fear. Dark means danger. Children frequently experience this fear, but with the help of understanding adults during this period, they learn to accept darkness.

In some cases vestiges of the fear remain and are carried into adulthood. Instead of admitting fear of darkness, the adult may try to avoid being ridiculed by saying, "I don't like to drive at night, the lights of the other cars bother me" or "I leave a light on all night because the dark upsets my dog." We may laugh at a childish and irrational fear of the dark but become just as disturbed ourselves over other unknowns that sometimes frighten us.

A young retail salesman came to me because his fear was making him physically ill. Conversation revealed that new owners had bought the store where he worked and he was afraid he would lose his job. The only basis for his fear was a chance remark he had overheard that the new owners would probably make some changes. The new owners simply represented to him an unknown quantity, and he was not able to deal calmly or rationally with unknowns.

He had to learn that the unknown is like a dark room and only needs light to dispel the fear. Reason and logic are ways of putting light into that room. Most fears are illogical and when you look at them analytically, you can see the fallacy within each fear.

Other Sources of Fear

Another source of fear for many people is their health. Again we are talking about irrational fear.

Without any symptoms and in spite of their physician's assurances, a man fears he will drop dead of a heart attack or a woman that she will develop cancer or suffer disability in an auto accident. Usually such health fears are disguised fear of disfigurement or death. A person will rarely say, "I'm afraid of death," but he will say, "I am afraid of getting pneumonia or a blood clot."

Fear related to health is often caused by a lack of confidence, both in oneself and one's place in the world. Building up a healthy self-esteem as well as a hope in the goodness and providence of God is one of the most effective means for banishing such fears.

Fear of failure is another prevalent cause of anxiety. We live in a work-oriented civilization which stresses success. Often the fear of failure is engendered in childhood. Parents and other adults may exert tremendous pressure upon a child to setting high and sometimes unrealistic standards. As a result he has a constant fear of failure which may give him some very concrete symptoms such as ulcers, sleeplessness or chronic indigestion. He may say that hard work is causing his ulcers, but the real cause is his fear of failure.

Dealing With Fear

Whatever your fears, you can learn to handle them. We saw the first step in the process in the case of the salesman who had groundless fears about losing his job. He admitted to himself that he was indeed afraid. Honestly facing up to your fears is the first step in overcoming them. Admitting that a fear exists does not mean giving in to it. Quite the opposite. Putting it in terms of a battle again, refusing to admit fear means that fear has you on the run. You won't even face up and fight.

Pretending that you are not afraid does not lessen the intensity of the fear but magnifies it. The unadmitted fear grows in importance in your life and can eventually be so overwhelming that it prevents you from acting. You are so terrified of snakes that you absolutely refuse to go camping. If you can turn around, so to speak, and look directly at your fear, you will find it to be smaller than you thought.

After admitting that you are afraid, the next step is to analyze your fear. When does this fear bother me most? Does it vary in intensity according to circumstances? Is there anything that I can do that lessens its intensity? Can I figure out where this fear started in my life?

Frightening childhood experiences frequently are the cause of adult fears. One interesting case was a man who was afraid to drive a car. He had an irrational fear that he would suddenly lose his mind while he was driving and forget how to operate the vehicle. "I am afraid that this might cause a terrible accident and kill some innocent people," he explained.

An intelligent man who was tops in his profession, he had no signs of any deterioration of his memory or mental abilities, yet he had been haunted by this fear since adolescence. It took many sessions before we were able to trace this fear to a traumatic child-

hood episode. As a boy he had been injured in a
car accident which occurred because his father was
driving while intoxicated. In his mind his drunken
father became transformed into a driver who had
suffered a sudden loss of memory. As a child he had
been unable to face the face that a loved parent
would endanger his life in this way. The incident
remained in his unconscious and continued to
trouble him even after he became an adult. In a
sense he was still reenacting that episode and trying to take the blame away from his father.

In looking for the root of our fears, we'll discover
that we have inherited some of them. In talking
with people who are afraid of storms, I have found
that most of them came from homes in which one
or both parents were afraid of storms and commu-
nicated this fear to their children.

Or sometimes our fear is just "borrowed." "I was
never afraid of flying until this new girl came to
work," Susan said, "but she has talked so much
about air crashes that now I'm afraid to fly." We
can also borrow fears about not being able to get
along with a certain associate because others tell
us how hard he is to deal with. An older brother or
sister can so harp on the difficulties of a course like
chemistry that a younger child may refuse to take
it. When we realize that we have just borrowed a
fear, we should throw it away as we would anything that is not useful to us. The old saying,
"Don't borrow trouble," can also be written,
"Don't borrow fears."

Talking Out Fears

We may be able to analyze our fears by ourselves. If we are honest with ourselves, we may be able to figure out the what and whys. But often it is more helpful to talk out your fear with a trusted friend, your parish priest or a family doctor. By doing so you are facing your fear directly and not letting it haunt your unconscious. The other person can help you sort out your feelings and ideas so that you'll have more insights into yourself.

It is axiomatic that you cannot solve the present fear until you clear up the past cause. Sometimes this may take professional help and counseling. In my practice I have dealt with many such cases and found that most of them responded in time to careful and sympathetic probing into the past. Once the cause was understood, it could be relegated to the past where it belonged.

An added way of coping with fear that many have found very successful is prayer. In talking to God people admit their fears and begin to face them. They ask for the calmness necessary to cope with them and trust in the strength that they will receive from a Father in heaven who loves them.

Especially in regard to fear of death, belief in God and prayer is helpful. Christ himself, the night before he died, talked about his fears and anxiety and expressed confidence in his Father. Those who believe in God's loving providence can trustingly leave to the Father those things they cannot control themselves. On the front of the mantel in the

ancient Hind's Head Hotel in Bray, England, is
written, "Fear knocked at the door. Faith answered.
No one was there."

We all need the confidence not to panic when fear
grips our hearts. We can face fear and win. In 1933,
Franklin D. Roosevelt encouraged a frightened
United States by saying in his inaugural address:
"The only thing we have to fear is fear itself."

Dealing With Your Anger

We all feel anger. Some of us face up to it, others try to hide it—even from themselves. The intensity as well as the control differs from person to person. But this emotion flares up within all of us, and a great measure of our happiness depends on how successfully we have learned to deal with it.

Anger is a paradoxical and complex emotion. It can be a positive force (perhaps better called *moral indignation*) used to protect another or right an injustice. More often it is a negative force which wrecks a project, a business, a life, a family. And even positive anger, although justified in cause, can be tainted in motive or excessive in expression.

Anger can flare up on the spur of the moment or be nurtured for a week or a year. Our anger can be open and visible to all or it can smolder undetected beneath the surface. Here I want to focus on how to deal with negative or destructive anger which occasionally burns within each of us.

Once we have made up our minds to control our anger rather than be controlled by it, I recommend a three-step program for mastering temper. The first step deals with causes, the second with consequences, and the third with practical means.

Facing Up to Anger

The first step in dealing with our anger is to face up to it and find the real causes. All of us are tempted to point the finger at everything and everyone but ourselves. We are willing to analyze what triggered the tantrums of other people but shy away from discussing our own. But the cure must start with ourselves. Alone or with the help of someone else, we must try to identify the cause of our wrath; we must distinguish between surface or contributing causes and the perhaps hidden but real source of our anger.

The surface causes are those most easily seen and recognized. A husband's lateness for supper may be the surface cause of a wife's pique, but the real reason may be resentment over what she sees as his failure to do his fair share as a parent.

An office manager was plagued with angry exchanges between his workers over seemingly trivial matters. A consulting psychologist pointed out to him that by trying to use every foot of office space, he had crowded his personnel. They felt on top of one another. When they were given more room, the quarrels ceased and there was a general atmosphere of helpfulness and consideration in the office.

The same thing can happen when family members are too crowded. They get on each other's nerves and fights are frequent. Even if the family cannot move to a larger house, just admitting that the overcrowding is a source of tension may help. Then efforts can be made for various members of the family to get away by themselves. A mother home all day in close quarters with small children may need a regular evening out with her bridge club and chances to shop alone.

As we noted in Chapter II, we often transfer anger from the real cause, perhaps a broken TV or a discouraging situation, to a person. A mother who has had trouble with her washing machine may severely scold her son for tracking in mud, when actually she is more angry at her washer than at him. The boss who has car trouble on the freeway will come to work already angry, and the first employee who comes into his office may receive a reprimand.

Not knowing what a person is really angry about is a source of great confusion to others, especially to children. One time a boy spreads his erector set all over the living room floor and his father comes and helps him build a skyscraper. Two days later the child does the same thing and his father, who is in a bad mood, angrily orders him to "get that junk out of the living room."

Hidden Causes of Anger

Marriage partners may also suffer from the same
anxiety of trying to guess what it is that makes a
spouse short-tempered. A woman patient complained to me, "I can never be sure how my husband is going to react. Sometimes he will scold me
for doing some small thing or buying something,
and then at other times he just shrugs and says
nothing. I know I would be far less nervous if I had
some way of knowing which things would make
him angry and which things would please him."

As it turned out, her husband was unaware of the
effect of his conduct on his wife. He didn't think
he was showing any particular anger toward her.
He admitted to being so worried about his business
that at times his anger would explode for little
reason. His wife could see the apparent causes for
his anger, but she was unaware of the hidden cause—
his work situation.

Hidden causes for anger include anxiety, worry,
frustration, disappointments, guilt, pain, sleeplessness, fatigue, depression and stress. Many people
are slow to admit that any of the above are the real
causes of their anger. They prefer to blame other
people or circumstances. Sadly, by not facing the
cause, they just worsen the situation.

Johnny did poorly on a school test. He came home
angry with himself because he knew he could have
done better if he had studied the night before. But
because anger with oneself is always difficult to
maintain, he vented his anger on his little brother.
A family fight was soon in process and his mother

had to step in and separate the boys. "I can't get along with him," complained Johnny. But what he should have said was, "I can't get along with myself."

A teacher who had a severe headache all day is an example of the vicious circle into which anger can lead us. During the last classroom period when a few of the children became restless, she angrily assigned a large punishment to the whole class. Then she felt bad not only because of the headache but for taking out her frustration on all the pupils. The teacher's guilt may well lead her to a new outburst of temper. Getting angry is a way of covering up that insistent voice within us that is telling us we have done wrong. Rather than expiating for the guilt, getting angry just adds to it.

Gauging the Consequences

Once we have faced up to the real causes, the second step is to realistically assess the consequences of our anger. Negative anger costs us emotionally, physically and practically. Reckoning the costs should give us added motivation for mastering our senseless emotion.

Anger can so dominate us that all our more tender and positive emotions of compassion, joy and hope are blocked out of our life. We can become bitter and cynical and despondent. Our ability to be objective or make logical decisions is diminished or destroyed. "Anger deprives a sage of his wisdom, a prophet of his vision," the Talmud says. The conclusions we reach in anger often are false, irrelevant or entirely erroneous. Our emotions block out the

the knowledge we may have of the truth. Reality is distorted so that we may not only be "seeing through a glass darkly," but we may not really be seeing at all. It is a sobering thing to realize later that you will have to abide by a decision you made in the heat of your anger.

A father once confided to me that in a fit of anger he had ordered his 17-year-old son out of the house. "I lost my head," the father admitted. "I didn't really mean for him to leave, but when I realized what I had said, it was too late. He was gone."

In this case, as in so many others, anger creates practical havoc. Fits of temper can damage family, social and work relationships and can interfere with one's role as parent, marriage partner, employee or employer, visitor or host. Anger can keep you from effective communication with others. It can lead to alienation from your children and relatives. It is a frequent cause of separations and divorces. Being hotheaded will keep us from getting coveted invitations, desired promotions or raises.

Also to be counted among the practical consequences of anger is the damage done when one is enraged. This may include bodily harm to others or to yourself as well as property damages. The man or woman who becomes angry, picks up a vase or a dish and smashes it will have to face the broken pieces later. They may unfortunately symbolize a broken marriage or friendship. You can't laugh away bruises or broken bones after a tantrum. It's no use to say, "I didn't mean it," because at the time you did.

Damaging Your Health

The third consequence of anger is the damage you can do to your health. Tests have shown that when a person becomes angry there are corresponding body changes. The heartbeat becomes more rapid, breathing frequency increases, tremors and muscular contractions occur and there is a change in body temperature and coloring.

Patients who were studied for their anger reactions reported their feelings in these words: "I felt cold all over and I couldn't seem to move." "I was so angry I just shook and afterward I felt tired and weak." "I got cold and then hot, my voice shook and I started to cry." Another patient said, "My heart was beating so hard I thought it would stop. I had chest pains afterward and couldn't seem to get my breath."

Self-injury frequently accompanies violent outbursts of anger. Bone doctors can tell you of people who have broken bones by smashing their hands against a wall or hitting a table in anger, or broken a toe by kicking a power mower that refused to start.

Such self-injury is sometimes the result of a repressed desire for self-punishment. The individual realizes that his anger is wrong, and even while he is expressing it he tries to punish himself for such violent feelings. Some people feel so remorseful over fits of anger directed against a loved one that they cannot conceive of not being punished. Whenever one of my patients quarreled with his wife, he

had an accident of some kind. The seriousness of
the accident was directly related to the intensity
of the quarrel.

Becoming the Master of Your Anger

After recognizing the true cause of our anger and
realistically surveying what it costs us physically,
practically and emotionally, we should be ready
for the third step of taking specific measures to
make ourselves the master of our anger rather than
its slave.

If our anger is with another individual, a good first
practical step is to muster up courage to discuss the
matter with him or her. We go not to attack him
but to clear up any misunderstandings and maybe
to frankly reveal to him how his actions bother us.
He may not realize this. A wife may think that her
husband prefers to take the car to the service sta-
tion himself, but he may resent frequently finding
the tank near empty when he is in a hurry to get to
work.

If you sincerely present your anger as *your* problem, something that is causing you distress, and ask
the other person's help in dealing with it, he or she
may be willing to cooperate or stop the irritating
conduct. William Blake sums it up well:
"I was angry with my friend:
I told my wrath, my wrath did end.
I was angry with my foe:
I told it not, my wrath did grow."

There are times, of course, when the direct
approach to the person causing your anger is

impossible or proves fruitless. Then, so that your wrath does not grow, it is helpful to discuss the whole matter with a noninvolved party who can mirror your true feelings back to you. This may help you see more clearly what is the real cause of your anger, and just talking about it may defuse the intensity of your emotion. Also, it may put the whole situation in perspective. Maybe you will conclude that although your anger is truly justified, the matter is really too insignificant to take away your peace of mind.

You may also get help in setting up realistic goals for conquering your temper. If you have identified the cause, you can also analyze the time and circumstances when you are tempted to lose your temper. So instead of resolving, "I am no longer going to get angry," you can say, "When I start discussing politics with my brother-in-law, I'm going to be on guard."

Or a mother, realizing that she usually gets most upset in the rush of getting husband off to work and children to school, can resolve that especially from 7:30 to 8 a.m. she will try to keep her cool.

A supervisor may realize that every week as it grows nearer the shipping deadline, he blows up more frequently. He resolves to schedule better and to be forewarned against flying off the handle under pressure.

Knowing Your "Early Warning" Signs

Even when you cannot foresee an explosive situation, you can learn to identify your anger "trigger

symptoms." These are signs which alert you that
your emotions are taking over. The trigger symptoms will naturally vary with individuals, but there
are a number which are fairly common anger warn-
ings: a sensation of muscular tightness, sudden
feelings of warmth or cold, trembling hands or
voice tremors, tears or breathing changes.

Any of these signs are like an indicator that there's
bad weather expected. One of the best gauges is
your voice. When you hear that first note of irritation, you know it is time to do something to stop
a potential explosion.

Then you can put on your emotional brakes,
change your mental environment by quickly thinking of something different and, if possible, something pleasant and relaxing. If you can, walk away
from the situation, change the topic of conversation
or just stop talking. Make yourself take a cooling-
off period.

I have known people to use these anger alert signs
in a variety of ways. One man said he always imagined that he was being photographed by a hidden
camera. "It made me stop and think," he said. "I
decided I wouldn't want to be caught behaving and
looking like a spoiled child."

So there are ways of dealing with anger, and we
should be convinced that we can control it in our
lives. As the Bible says in the Book of Proverbs,
"The quick-tempered man makes a fool of himself,
but the prudent man is at peace" (Proverbs 15:17).

Overcoming Loneliness

"I Want to Be Alone "

That of course is the badge of identity of Greta Garbo, one of the most famous actresses of our century. In her particular case the statement apparently signifies a wish for withdrawal from the unacceptable tensions of fame in our modern society.

Some people may say "I want to be alone" when really they are pouting and saying in effect, "You have hurt my feelings and therefore I want nothing to do with you." For others it could be the external sign of depression. "I feel preoccupied with sadness and have no energy left for you." In more mature personalities the desire to be alone can be healthy because the time apart is used to read or meditate or pray.

Ordinarily, however, most of us would have to say, "I do *not* want to be alone." Yet even though we worked to make ourselves enjoyable to be with, and have developed solid friendships with relatives and others, many of us are destined to spend a good number of years alone—and too often lonely. I will expand on that point later, but let me make it clear at the beginning there are solutions to the loneliness problem.

Basically what is being described above is what philosophers label an *existentialist situation*. I think it will be profitable for us to briefly define and examine this current philosophy.

Existentialism concentrates on the *immediate*; the time is *now* and the place is *here*. An existentialist might say, "There is no answer as to why I exist and my creation is an accident. There is no intrinsic meaning to my being and my specific presence on earth is an absurdity. I am the only point of reference for my world and I am anguished by this awareness of my solitary situation. In short, I am alone."

This is a superficial, though I think accurate, picture of the most popular philosophy of our century. It is also an attitude or belief which in one form or another is far more prevalent than one would at first suppose.

The dropout says, "Society stinks. I will have no part of government, business, education or military." Once he finds himself thus "tuned in" he then "drops out." At this point he is a true existentialist character; having previously found his justification for being in terms of society, by rejecting it he is now alone.

It is obviously unbearably painful, however, for the dropout to be alone, so he quickly joins company with a like group of sufferers and forms a new society in order to relieve his anguish. In this new group the standards and mores of society are discarded, but only while the group is together. Some of the hippies of the 1960's have now left the counterculture and abandoned its ways of speech and dress for more average ways of speaking and dressing.

Not that the hippies didn't have something to say. None of it was very original but they did speak of love, oneness of humanity, acceptance of sexuality, discarding of senseless materialism and hypocritical nationalism. However, often their talk of love came across as unreal. Their wish for oneness with others applied to their in-group only.

A contradiction of thought versus action can be found in most of their positions. They sounded good and within the basic Christian context were good, but the hippie in his bizarre isolation from society only frightened adults who needed to be stimulated to self-examination, and deceived many young people into believing that some very dangerous chemicals (e.g., LSD) can create wisdom. In a study for one of our medical journals, I observed that to compensate for their lack of creativity, wisdom and productivity they took drugs that made them feel creative and significant.

On the whole, the hippie movement was a negative solution to the existentialist problem of, "I am alone."

Coping With Loneliness

Others besides hippies, of course, try to escape through drugs or alcohol. These are extreme ways of dealing with "I can't stand being alone and feeling meaningless."

Now hardly any of these people—and their numbers are huge—know that they are negative existentialist characters, but nonetheless they are and we will label them as such for sake of convenience. Their solution is what the same philosophers would describe as inauthentic: an escape rather than a coming to grips. They are people in crisis who have been panicked into a false solution in order to avoid the even more painful realization of their basic aloneness.

As you can easily see this philosophy is not some vague intellectual exercise designed to bore college students but is indeed very real and very painful. And so that it does not reach too far beyond your interests, let us bring it back to the more common and practical plane.

For example, if you are an elderly woman you will probably spend the last portion of your life alone. If you are married, your husband probably will be dead for the final decade of your existence and your children will for the most part be absent from your everyday activities for a quarter of a century. If you are an unmarried career woman, you will not only have neither mate nor family but you will also not be gainfully employed for close to 20 years. If either of these situations is yours, you may be destined for a depressing sense of "not belonging" and a long painful period of loneliness—no one to cook for, work for or care for.

If you are a man who has been devoted to work and family, the situation will be no better. Not only may you be forced into an early retirement, but even before that your working week may become progressively shorter as a result of technological "progress." Your education has been almost totally oriented to your work.

Faced with much leisure time and a premature retirement, you may have nothing more to do in your comfortable modern home than view endless hours of increasingly boring television. Your children will have been long ago grown up and gone. At least you will have the comfort of your wife's companionship—if during your busy career you have taken time to form such a relationship with her. Your culture will promote recreational activities to fill your time, but you will find this only occasional relief. For play without meaningful work soon becomes stale.

Some Alternatives to Loneliness

I can assure you that I am not depicting this certain shape of the grim things to come in order to disturb you. Being a healer of distressed minds, it is just as unhappy a task for me to set these things down as it is for you to read them. Nor are they in any way exaggerated or distorted. For those who may doubt the accuracy of this prediction, I invite you to visit one of our typical retirement cities and see for yourself.

Is then the inevitable outcome of a life alone a lonely death? If this were the only ultimate solution, I would not be so unkind as to describe it. Rather, permit me to demonstrate some alternatives.

A once extremely active business executive found himself at the age of 60 bumped from his job into lucrative retirement. Two weeks of playing golf and not shaving and he was literally going out of his skull. Things at home were no better. Most of his and his wife's social life had in later years revolved around his business. Earlier their mutual interests had focused on their three children, who had long since moved to other parts of the country. Despite being still very vigorous, he could find absolutely nothing useful to do in his efficient industrial community. And his wife found progressively irritating his lying around the house doing nothing.

However, they loved one another too well to sustain this sterile vacuum for 10 years. So next thing you know, to the consternation of family and friends, they sold their now tomb-like home and belongings and were off together for the Peace Corps. "At their age, they must be nuts," was the response of many of their acquaintances.

Nonetheless, two years later when I encountered them in Puerto Rico they were suntanned,

delightedly working together and intensely
involved in teaching some farmers how to better
irrigate their crops as well as build hygenic outdoor
latrines. They had learned a new language and culture, a new way of life and a new way of happiness.
Their solution was not existential despair or retreat
into loneliness and solitude.

Mrs. L., a widow of two years, was for some
months recovered from her acute and normal
period of grief. She felt and was so alone that she
would sit for hours "listening to the awesome
sound of complete silence." Her life with a rather
gruff and feelingless husband had hardly been fulfilling. They had had little in common other than
the children and even in this area were usually at
odds as regards home rules, discipline and such.
She had gone through a similar depression when
her youngest had departed for college. However,
a year of this loneliness was enough for her. She
decided to find something to do with her child-
barren hours.

This was not as simply done, for she had relatively
little formal education, despite the fact that she
was quite interested in world and community
affairs. In order that she have some skill, she
attended morning classes at a business college and
quickly learned office procedure. Within a month
she was working afternoons as a receptionist for
the local pediatrician. That was when she was 40.

Now she was 60 and felt too old and a little too
tired for the doctor's busy office. With her training,
job experience and interest it was really no problem. Her pastor quickly found her a part-time job

as secretary for the nearby Catholic Maternity Institute, where she could also share the anticipatory joys of the young mothers-to-be.

These are but two examples from life of positive ways of handling the problem of being alone. There are many others. Mrs. L. could just as easily have become a practical nurse, which many middle-aged women do.

To be alone is not necessarily the tragedy that the drug addict or alcoholic make it. It can be an opportunity for further growth, satisfaction and fulfillment. Many people, from necessity, spend most of their lives doing tasks they are either bored with or even hate. Being alone is a second chance to do other things. You didn't want to be a salesman but an artist? Now that you have so much time on your hands I hope that over the years you have kept up on your sketching, taken an occasional evening painting class and followed the contemporary collection at the museum. Your hands are therefore not too rusty. So now you'll quickly become deeply involved in a set of canvasses you've spent 20 years thinking about.

You're sick of the bridge-club, coffee-sip circuit? The chatter is superficial and your two years of college are wasted there? You have no idea how desperately they need a CCD teacher for 20 Catholic children scattered throughout a fragmented ghetto.

You're lonely yourself but are sensitive to other people's loneliness? Select a local old folks' home and make regular visits to these usually otherwise abandoned individuals.

You enjoy good health and are thankful for it, but pained by all the afflicted in our world? Discover what deep ties can be established by reading to a blind person or going to the trouble of learning sign language and working with the deaf.

I can promise you that I could easily list another one hundred meaningful solutions to the despair of being alone, and I don't mean just busy-busy work either: the teacher's corps, apostolic works in multitude; personal opportunities to complete an education, learn a new skill; serious reading, meditation. I mean desperately needed and potentially immensely gratifying involvements.

And the latter is precisely the clue—involvement. If you have any real interest or love for any one person or persons, existential despair need not be your fate. Camus, a great French philosopher and writer, found life so "absurd" that he became profoundly preoccupied with death and wrote a brilliant essay on the meaning of suicide. Eventually he came to see that love, for another person and humanity, was his only answer to existential despair.

When one loves generously, it is impossible to suffer loneliness to any large extent. A psychoanalyst might put it this way: the turning in on oneself of love and aggression leads to painful unrealistic self-love, a sense of isolation and depression. The turning outward of love and aggression fulfills the internal need to enjoy others and work. Meaningful discharge of these needs, in turn, leads to a realistic sense of self-worth.

Many scholars suggest that Christ is history's best example of an existential character fulfilled. Certainly his message of love has been the greatest and most successful salve for the wounds of despair.

His teachings challenge us to love and commit ourselves to one another.

And incidentally, I can absolutely say from my clinical experience that those who find loneliness the easiest to resolve are those sincere Christians I have seen who have previously spent a lifetime maturing such an attitude of commitment. They have already been authentic people in the past and thus look forward to any opportunity for aloneness so that they may find new ways to express their love. There are other ways to develop such an attitude, to be sure. But the greatest message ever told is available and accessible to all.

Loneliness does not have to destroy us. It can be the spark for developing hidden talents and tapping unused inner resources.

How to Live
With a Neurotic

It ain't easy! If by chance your wife, husband, friend or business associate is unfortunate enough to be among the one out of every 10 Americans (a conservative estimate) who is suffering from a mental disturbance, you have a most difficult problem to deal with. And in most cases, you *do* have to deal with at least one neurotic person.

Surely it is hard enough just to master the anxieties of everyday living in our sometimes frantic and normally complicated world. These practical and specific daily problems are a challenge for anyone to handle. Add to them the demands of fathering or mothering and of working to support a family, and you see the strain under which many people work. These are not simple tasks in a society as unstable and materialistically oriented as ours.

If one adds to this the misfortune of having to live and cope with a partner, relative or other intimate person who is neurotic, life can easily seem either unbearable or impossible. For although the actions of the ill person toward you may seem very peculiar, the reasons for such behavior are either a complete mystery or, at best, extremely elusive.

For example, your once loving husband and the attentive father to your children now comes home each evening complaining that he is too tired to listen to your problems of the day and too irritable to lovingly discipline some minor misbehavior of one of the children. He rarely wishes to take you out anymore and spends most of Sunday snoozing on the couch with the T.V. going full blast. He ends the day by blaming his whole bad week on the fact that the potatoes at dinner were not hot enough. He follows this gripe by provoking a petty quarrel with you and then sulks for three days. When he does muster up enough energy to converse, it is only to whine about how he hates his work, has no friends and feels that his sole function in life is to support ingrates. Poor guy. Poor you, too.

Perhaps a wife endlessly chatters about a dozen trivial social activities she recently has become involved in. None of this busy, busy preoccupation amounts to very much and the detailed amount of it is actually quite boring to you after a hard day's work. On top of this, that's the third tasteless frozen dinner you've had this week. When you finally crawl into bed your wife is suddenly "too tired" to enjoy sex with you. In addition the house is always a mess, and she forgot to pick up your shirts from the laundry. When you, with slight irritation, finally inquire as to what's she been doing with all her time, she accuses you of being an unfeeling brute and bursts into tears.

Over a period of time and after a number of repetitions, the healthy partner comes to realize that something is very much wrong with his or her spouse. Hopefully, this suspicion has or will be supported by some objective third party: the parish priest, some spiritual or lay counselor or the family physician.

Temporary Problem

Perhaps it is a situational problem; that is, one that is temporary and related to a specific crisis point in life.

For the man it may be his 40th birthday and the realization that he will always be doing exactly what he is doing now. He is finding it hard to face the fact that he will never be a foreman or a vice-president.

The married woman will have to learn that life is not over now that the youngest child has started grade school. She will also come to the realization that getting involved in a multitude of meaningless activities will not make her day rich and fulfilling.

These are typical situational problems. There are a number of them. They should not be confused with time and curable by rational thought or advice. A couple's initial love for one another at this stage can take on new meaning. Together they can re-orient their goals and needs to further growth and different kinds of fulfillment.

What Is a Neurosis?

Neuroses, the symptoms of two varieties of which were described in the first examples, are irrational. They are emotional conflicts that have no basis in current-day events nor are they materially affected by logical considerations or loving reassurance.

Once you are convinced that your loved one is a neurotic, you will probably take the matter to that "objective third party" mentioned earlier. He will usually offer several courses of action. The disturbed individual will be confronted with the painful fact that he or she is emotionally ill. He will be assured that with proper psychological or psychiatric help he stands a very good chance of recovering. Depending upon the nature and severity of the problem, he will then be referred for some type of drug therapy, short-term psychotherapy ranging from one to a dozen talking visits, or in some cases for psychoanalysis.

Once Therapy Starts

Convincing your spouse to seek professional aid is not the end of your difficulties. Once the therapy has begun, you may expect little if any communication or advice from the doctor. Confidentiality is the cornerstone of treatment with a neurotic, and the family will rarely be brought into the case. The patient will no doubt bring up his treatment from time to time. Just listen.

Controlling your natural curiosity and tendency to
give advice is especially necessary when the patient
develops toward the therapist the same hostile attitude he once had toward you. Such hostility is a
sign of progress, for those negative feelings are
part of his problem and belong in the doctor's
office. You can take comfort because the doctor is
getting those feelings off your back.

In the Meantime

What do you do in the meantime to live with a neurotic? I will now attempt to explore the two chief
reasons why I said, "It ain't easy." One is the patient's fault, and the other is yours. I use the term
"fault," of course, not in the sense of blame but
merely to indicate which party is creating some
undesirable effect.

First of all, the neurotic is not reacting in terms of
the here and now. Rather, he is repeating some old
painful emotional conflict from childhood which
remained unsolved at that time and is rearing its
ugly head in the present. All of the original drama
is recreated. Only the staging and costuming are
changed to make the script modern and convincing.

The "weary husband" was originally a depressed
boy. He feels unloved by you just as he felt unloved by his unaffectionate mother. And he pro-
vokes the same argument with you over dinner as
his father regularly did with his mother.

The "busy wife" cannot find anything meaningful
to do. As a child she showed early signs of having
unusual creative gifts as well as a precocious intelli-

gence. Her father squelched these, informing her that a woman's role in life was only to take care of a family. "Keep busy and stay out of trouble," he always told her. Her current attitude toward sex comes from an identification with her sexually frigid mother.

These are greatly oversimplified dynamics of neuroses, but they will serve to make my point; namely, it is almost impossible to deal with a current-day reality when one is living in the past. The healthy wife of the neurotic is the unfortunate object of ancient history, which usually has nothing whatsoever to do with her basic personality. This phenomenon is called transference. Old childhood attitudes are transferred onto present-day figures, regardless of reality. Inevitably this transference is to whomever the patient is closest. There is always such a massive force behind this transference that reason will not prevail. Only a professional uprooting and thorough exploration of the original events with a discharge of all the associated painful feelings will relieve the situation. This is the neurotic's "fault."

Don't Play Along With the Neurosis

The healthy spouse's "fault" is intimately connected with and inseparable from the neurotic's cause. The spouse allows himself or herself to be put into a position that is not true. For example, if you are not a bad cook, why permit yourself to become upset and angry at your husband's accusation that you are? Likewise, if you are not "an unfeeling brute" why get angry when your emotionally ill wife rejects a reasonable sexual overture on your part?

One sees at once what a delicate situation can develop in living with neurotics. On the one hand they need you to act with them within their illness. And on the other they play into forces within you that are, after all, only human. It may also seem a trifle harsh to inform someone you love that:

1. "What you are experiencing has nothing to do with me."

2. "You had better take this up with a cold-hearted professional stranger."

However, painful as it may be, such directness is necessary. You neither created the neurosis, nor are you capable of solving it. To be kind and gentle in confronting such a person is one thing. To be indirect or play into his drama is a disservice to you both.

In the end, one does not after all live with a neurotic but rather creates an atmosphere and an attitude which will foster his overcoming his illness. "It ain't easy," but the approach outlined here is ultimately an expression of the greatest love for all concerned.

A Word for the Road

I'm glad that you've stayed with me in taking a
quick look at ways you can make life happier for
yourself and your family. The fact that you've
invested time in this book is an indication that you
have the desire and drive necessary for a happy
trip through life. I hope you continue your journey
with these convictions.

I can better my life. You must have confidence
that you can master your anger. You can face up
to your fears and win. You can overcome loneliness. You can take action to get help for a neurotic
member of your family. In short, you can deepen
your friendship with yourself and your family.

I must start. You must take the initiative. You cannot wait for someone else to make you happy. Certainly you need other people. You may need help from a professional. You have to take the first step or make the first phone call.

Now is the time. I hope that you've gotten some helpful insights in this book. Act on them now. Don't stew in your discomfort and keep putting off what you know will make you happier.

Growing is a lifelong adventure. You are setting out not on an overnight trip but a lifetime journey. You won't be disappointed that tomorrow and next week and next month you are still on the way. Growing in friendship with yourself and your family is the adventure of your life. There are no simple gimmicks, no instant growth or effortless success. But your peace and joy deepen as you come closer and closer to self-acceptance and shared love with others.

Give it your best and enjoy the excitement and rewards of the journey!

SBN 33-4 $1.35

Dr. Jean Rosenbaum

Nationally known author/psychiatrist Jean Rosenbaum turns his attention to the primary relationship in our lives: the family.

How do we begin to improve the relationships between ourselves and our spouses, our parents, our children, our brothers and sisters? We begin by improving our relationship with <u>ourselves.</u>

"Yes," reaffirms Dr. Rosenbaum, "it is healthy to like yourself. For if you don't like yourself you will find that it's impossible to live with anyone else."

In direct and simple language, the author goes on to give step-by-step specifics for expanding and enjoying family life—for better understanding the people whose lives are closest to our own.

The author invites us to experience and share this "friendly handbook" pointing the way to:

- Living with yourself and liking it
- Coping with your fears, anger, loneliness and conflict
- Being friends with your family

ABOUT THE AUTHOR: Jean Rosenbaum, M.D., is a celebrated psychiatrist, lecturer, artist and author. He has appeared on such shows as <u>Merv Griffin,</u> the <u>Dinah Shore Show,</u> the <u>Today Show</u> and the <u>Tonight Show,</u> and has been interviewed in over 200 newspapers and magazines. Also the author of numerous articles for professional journals, his books include <u>Becoming Yourself</u> and the national bestseller <u>Is Your VW a Sex Symbol?</u> Dr. Rosenbaum currently practices psychiatry in Durango, Colorado.

St. Anthony Messenger Press, 1615 Republic St., Cincinnati, OH 45210

What's God been doing all this time?

DAVID ALLAN HUBBARD